VEGETABLES
◆ ON THE GRILL ◆

Creative Cooking Library

By the Editors of Sunset Books

SUNSET BOOKS
President & Publisher: Susan J. Maruyama
Director, Finance & Business Affairs: Gary Loebner
Director, Manufacturing
& Sales Service: Lorinda Reichert
Director, Sales & Marketing: Richard A. Smeby
Director, New Business: Kenneth Winchester
Editorial Director: Bob Doyle
Developmental Editor: Lynne Gilberg

SUNSET PUBLISHING CORPORATION
Chairman: Jim Nelson
President/Chief Executive Officer: Robin Wolaner
Chief Financial Officer: James E. Mitchell
Publisher: Stephen J. Seabolt
Circulation Director: Robert I. Gursha
Editor, Sunset Magazine: William R. Marken
Senior Editor, Food & Entertaining: Jerry Anne Di Vecchio

All the recipes in this book were developed and tested in the
Sunset test kitchens. For information about any Sunset Book
please call 1-800-634-3095.

The nutritional data provided for each recipe is for a single
serving, based on the number of servings and the amount of each
ingredient. If a range is given for the number of servings and/or
the amount of an ingredient, the analysis is based on the average
of the figures given. The nutritional analysis does not include
optional ingredients or those for which no specific amount is
stated. If an ingredient is listed with a substitution, the data
was calculated using the first choice.

Nutritional analysis of recipes: Hill Nutrition
Associates, Inc. of Florida.

Sunset Creative Cooking Library
was produced by St. Remy Press

President: Pierre Léveillé
Managing Editor: Carolyn Jackson
Managing Art Director: Diane Denoncourt
Senior Editor: Elizabeth Cameron
Art Director: Chantal Bilodeau
Editorial Assistant: Jennifer Meltzer
Administrator: Natalie Watanabe
Production Manager: Michelle Turbide
System Coordinator: Éric Beaulieu
Proofreader: Veronica Schami
Indexer: Christine Jacobs

*The following persons also assisted in the preparation
of this book: Philippe Arnoldi, Maryse Doray, Lorraine Doré,
Dominique Gagné, Geneviève Monette.*

COVER: *Vegetables with Fresh Herbs (page 62)*

PHOTOGRAPHY
*Robert Chartier: 6, 7, 9; **Peter Christiansen:** 3, 12, 16, 20,
22, 24; **Norman A. Plate:** 32, 34; **Kevin Sanchez:** Cover, 10,
48; **Spathis & Miller:** 52; **E.K. Waller:** 56; **Darrow M. Watt:**
Inside cover; 4, 60; **Weber-Stephen Products Co.:** 5, 7, 9;
Tom Wyatt: 28, 44; **Nikolay Zurek:** 38.*

ILLUSTRATION
Sally Shimizu: 8.

Special thanks to Weber-Stephen Products Co., Palatine, Ill.

Table of Contents

Barbecuing Basics

Glistening with an aromatic herb baste, vegetables such as these are gaining favor as an alternative to traditional barbecue fare.

There are three main types of barbecues —charcoal-fired, gas, and electric— some of which are shown on the opposite page. Your choice will depend on where you'll use your barbecue, the number of people you'll be serving, and the kinds of food you're most likely to barbecue.

Charcoal-fired barbecues. The most popular models are open braziers, covered kettles, and boxes with hinged lids.

Open braziers vary from tabletop portables and hibachis to larger models. Many have a cooking grill that can be raised or lowered to adjust the distance between the charcoal and food.

Covered kettles have dampers on the lid and under the firebox to adjust the flow of air and control the heat. They may be used, uncovered or covered, for grilling over direct heat (*page 8*). Kettle barbecues are available in various sizes; the 18- to 24-inch-diameter models are the most popular.

Boxes with hinged lids are similar to covered kettles and can be used either covered for cooking by indirect heat or open or closed for grilling over direct heat.

Gas and electric barbecues. Outdoor units fueled by bottled gas usually roll on wheels; natural gas units are mounted on a fixed pedestal and are connected to a permanent gas line. Electric units are portable; they are plugged into the nearest outlet. All gas units and some electric models use a briquet-shaped material, such as lava rock, above the burner. When meat juices drip on these hot "briquets," smoke rises to penetrate and flavor the food.

Types of Barbecues

Gas barbecue

Charcoal-fired kettle

Portable charcoal-fired kettle

Direct gas barbecue

Portable gas barbecue

Charcoal, Starters & Fragrant Woods

Charcoal refers to the 2-inch pressed briquets, which may differ somewhat in density and composition. For best results, choose long-burning briquets, and ignite them using one of the following techniques.

Fire chimney. Stack briquets inside the chimney on top of wadded sheets of newspaper, then light. In about 30 minutes, you'll have burning coals ready to use; lift off the chimney and spread the hot coals.

Electric starter. This is one of the easiest and cleanest charcoal starters you can buy. Set the starter on a few briquets and pile more briquets on top; then plug in the starter. After 10 minutes, remove the starter from the pile; in about 20 more minutes, the coals will be ready.

Solid starter. These small, compressed, blocks or sticks light easily with a match and continue to burn until the coals are ready for cooking (about 30 minutes).

Propane starter. Simply stack the briquets around the burner; then light the burner and proceed as directed by the manufacturer.

Flavoring foods with the smoke of fragrant woods is an ancient cooking art still in style with modern patio chefs. Several popular fragrant woods are shown below.

Hickory chips

Charcoal

Mesquite chips

Basil wood chips

Barbecuing Tips

When preparing the recipes in this book, keep these tips in mind.

• The recipes were tested with the cooking grill 4 to 6 inches above the coals. If your grill is closer, the cooking time will be shorter.

• Use long-handled cooking tools to avoid burning yourself.

• Wear barbecue mitts for emergency adjustment of the grill and removal of drip pans from the fire bed.

• Use a water-filled spray bottle to extinguish flare-ups.

• Always turn food with long-handled tongs or a spatula—a long fork pierces food and allows juices to escape.

• Salt food *after* cooking (salt draws out juices).

• If using fragrant woods in a gas barbecue, the wood chips usually need to be contained in a pan and used according to the barbecue manufacturer's directions.

• Use small-mesh grills and baskets to keep small pieces of food, such as fish and vegetables from falling through the barbecue grill.

• Be sure that ashes are completely cold (sparks linger for many hours) before you dump ashes into a paper or plastic container.

Propane starter

Electric starter

Solid starter cubes

Chimney

Two Ways to Barbecue

Direct- or indirect-heat cooking techniques differ in how the coals are arranged and in whether the barbecue is covered. For direct-heat grilling, any barbecue is satisfactory; to cook by indirect heat, you'll need a model with a lid.

By direct heat. Open the bottom dampers if your barbecue has them; for a covered barbecue, remove or open lid. Spread briquets on the fire grate in a solid layer that's 1 to 2 inches bigger all around than the grill area required for the food. Then mound the charcoal and ignite it. When the coals reach

Direct heat   Indirect heat

the fire temperature specified in the recipe, spread them out into a single layer again. Set the grill at the recommended height above coals. Grease the grill, then arrange the food on the grill. To maintain an even heat, scatter 10 new briquets over the fire bed every 30 minutes.

By indirect heat. Open or remove the lid from a covered barbecue, then open the bottom dampers. Pile about 50 long-burning briquets on the fire grate and ignite them. Let the briquets burn until hot; this usually takes about 30 minutes. Using long-handled tongs, bank about half the briquets on each side of the fire grate; then place a metal drip pan in the center. Set the cooking grill 4 to 6 inches above the drip pan; lightly grease the grill. Set the food on the grill directly above the drip pan. Add 5 or 6 briquets to each side of the fire grate at 30- to 40-minute intervals to keep temperature constant.

Fire Temperature

Use the fire temperature recommended in the recipe.

Hot. You can hold your hand close to the grill for only 2 to 3 seconds. Coals are barely covered with gray ash.

Medium. You can hold your hand at grill level for 4 to 5 seconds. Coals glow red through a layer of gray ash.

Low. You can hold your hand at grill level for at least 6 to 7 seconds. Coals are covered with a thick layer of ash.

Barbecue Accessories

This array of barbecue accessories contains some of the new or updated equipment that outdoor chefs should have on hand. Protect your clothing by wearing an apron. A metal brush does a good job of cleaning the grill if it is still hot.

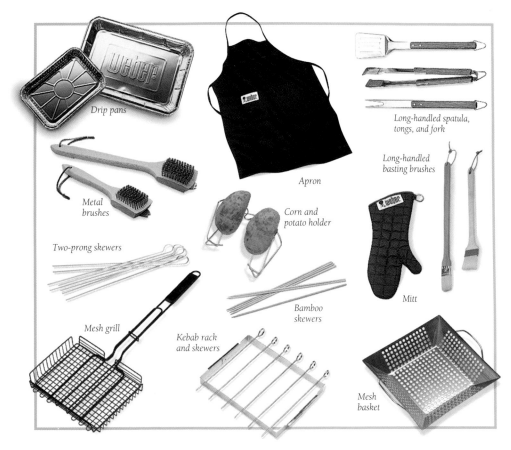

Drip pans

Long-handled spatula, tongs, and fork

Long-handled basting brushes

Apron

Metal brushes

Corn and potato holder

Two-prong skewers

Mitt

Mesh grill

Kebab rack and skewers

Bamboo skewers

Mesh basket

Grilling Fresh Vegetables

Before grilling, prepare vegetables as directed below. To keep vegetables moist as they cook, brush them with plain or seasoned butter or oil, or a basting sauce. Place large pieces directly on the grill; skewer smaller ones or use a mesh grill or basket. Cook on a lightly greased grill 4 to 6 inches above medium coals. Turn vegetables frequently.

Artichokes
Cut off top third. Trim stem, coarse outer leaves, and thorny tips. Rinse well, then plunge into acidulated water (3 tablespoons vinegar per quart of water). When all artichokes have been prepared, drain; then cook in boiling water to cover until stem end is tender when pierced (30 to 45 minutes). Drain; cut into halves lengthwise.
Grilling time: 5 to 8 minutes.

Beets
Scrub beets; trim tops 1 inch above stem end. When coals are coated with gray ash (about 30 minutes), mound briquets on one side of grate; add 8 briquets. Lay beets on grill, but not directly over coals. Cover barbecue and open dampers. After 30 minutes, add 6 more briquets.
Grilling time: About 45 minutes.

Bell peppers and fresh chiles
Rinse and pat dry.
Grilling time: 8 to 10 minutes.

Broccoli
Cut off tough stalk ends; peel tender stalks. Leave bunches whole; or, if thicker than 2 inches, cut in half lengthwise. Blanch for 2 to 3 minutes.
Grilling time: 4 to 6 minutes.

Cabbage and radicchio
Cut cabbage into quarters lengthwise. Cut radicchio into halves.
Grilling time: 6 to 10 minutes.

Carrots
Cook whole baby carrots or small regular carrots in boiling water to cover until just tender (5 to 10 minutes). Drain. Thread baby carrots on skewers.
Grilling time: 8 to 10 minutes.

Corn
Pull off dry outer husks until you reach light green inner husks; tear several outer husks into 1/4-inch strips to use as ties later. Gently pull back inner husks without tearing from cobs. Remove and discard silk. Spread corn with oil, butter, or baste. Lay inner husks back in place

around corn; tie with strips of husks at top to enclose. Immerse in cold water to cover for 15 to 30 minutes. Drain well.
Grilling time: 15 to 20 minutes.
Alternatively, peel off and discard all husks and silk.
Grilling time: About 8 minutes.

Eggplants
Cut off stem end of Oriental or small regular eggplants. Cut Oriental eggplants into halves lengthwise; cut regular eggplants lengthwise into 1½-inch-wide wedges.
Grilling time: 12 to 15 minutes.

Fennel
Cut off and discard woody stems. Cut vertically into 4 equal slices.
Grilling time: About 20 minutes.

Leeks
Trim root ends; trim tops, leaving 2 inches of green leaves. Split lengthwise to within ½ inch of root ends. Rinse well.
Grilling time: 4 to 6 minutes.

Mushrooms
Fresh: Cut off tough stem ends. Thread smaller mushrooms on skewers.
Dried: Soak in hot water to cover until soft, about 15 minutes. Squeeze out water; trim stems. Thread smaller mushrooms on skewers.
Grilling time: About 10 minutes.

Onions (dry)
Do not peel. Cut small onions into halves. Cut larger ones into quarters and thread on skewers, making sure onions lie flat.
Grilling time: 15 to 20 minutes.

Onions (green)
Trim root ends and 2 inches of green tops.
Grilling time: 6 to 8 minutes.

Potatoes, sweet potatoes, and yams
Cut small potatoes into halves. Cut large ones lengthwise into 1-inch-wide wedges. Cook in boiling water to cover until tender when pierced (6 to 8 minutes).
Grilling time: 8 to 10 minutes.

Squash (summer)
Leave small squash (1 inch or less in diameter) whole. Cut larger squash into halves lengthwise.
Grilling time: 10 to 15 minutes.

Tomatoes
Cut tomatoes into halves.
Grilling time: 8 to 12 minutes.

APPETIZERS & SALADS

*L*et your barbecue do double

duty by grilling fresh vegeta-

bles alongside a meat, fish, or

chicken entrée. It's an easy

way to add extra color, flavor,

and nutrition to grilled meals.

In this section, you'll find

tempting recipes for appetizers

and salads, as well as veg-

etable pizzas that are baked

to perfection on the grill.

GRILLED TOMATO & PESTO PIZZA, RECIPE ON PAGE 14
NECTARINE & BASIL PIZZA, RECIPE ON PAGE 15

Grilled Tomato & Pesto Pizza

(PICTURED ON PAGE 12 AT LEFT)

Cook these individually sized pizzas over medium heat;
if the coals are too hot, the crust will scorch.

◆

PER SERVING: *693 calories, 23 g protein, 62 g carbohydrates, 40 g total fat, 54 mg cholesterol, 947 mg sodium*

PREPARATION TIME: *45 min.*
GRILLING TIME: *15 min.*

1 *loaf frozen whole-wheat*
   or white bread dough,
   thawed
2 *Tbsp. olive oil*
4 *large Roma-type tomatoes,*
   cut lengthwise into
   ½-inch slices
8 *Tbsp. prepared pesto*
   sauce
2 *cups shredded*
   mozzarella cheese
Salt and pepper

On a floured board, divide and shape dough into 4 equal balls. Roll each into a 5- to 6-inch-wide round. Brush tops and bottoms with oil, set on foil, and flatten to ⅛ inch. Let rise, uncovered, at room temperature until slightly puffy (15 to 25 minutes).

Meanwhile, place tomato slices on a grill 4 to 6 inches above a solid bed of hot coals. Brown on both sides (about 5 minutes total). Set aside.

When coals are medium, flip dough onto the grill; peel off and discard foil. Cook until golden brown on bottom (2 to 3 minutes).

With a wide spatula, transfer dough to a 12- by 15-inch baking sheet, browned side up. Spread 2 tablespoons of pesto sauce on each bread round, and top with grilled tomato slices and mozzarella cheese.

Return to grill. Cover barbecue, open vents, and cook until topping is hot and bottom of bread is crisp and flecked with brown (3 to 4 minutes). Remove from grill; add salt and pepper to taste.

Makes 4 servings

Nectarine & Basil Pizza

(PICTURED ON PAGE 12 AT BOTTOM)

The unusual combination of nectarines and fresh basil makes an intriguing topping for these flat breads baked on the barbecue.

◆

PER SERVING: *714 calories, 26 g protein, 74 g carbohydrates, 37 g total fat, 53 mg cholesterol, 935 mg sodium*

PREPARATION TIME: *45 min.*
GRILLING TIME: *10 min.*

- 1 *loaf frozen whole-wheat or white bread dough, thawed*
- 4 *small, pitted firm-ripe nectarines, thinly sliced*
- 2 *tsp. balsamic or seasoned rice vinegar*
- 4 *tsp. olive oil*
- 1⅓ *cups shredded jack cheese*
- ½ *cup finely shredded Parmesan cheese*
- ½ *cup finely shredded fresh basil or 2 tsp. dry basil*
- 4 *Tbsp. pine nuts*

Prepare dough as in recipe opposite.

Meanwhile, in a nonreactive bowl, mix together nectarine slices with vinegar and olive oil.

Place dough on a grill 4 to 6 inches above a solid bed of medium coals; discard foil. Cook until golden brown on bottom (2 to 3 minutes).

With a wide spatula, transfer dough to a 12- by 15-inch baking sheet, browned side up. Top each bread round with ⅓ cup jack cheese and 2 tablespoons Parmesan. With a slotted spoon, scatter nectarines equally over each bread round and sprinkle each with basil and pine nuts.

Return to grill. Cover barbecue, open vents, and cook until topping is hot and bottom of bread is crisp and flecked with brown (3 to 4 minutes). Remove from grill; add salt and pepper to taste.

Makes 4 servings

Eggplant Salad with Red Peppers

__H__eat from the grill
intensifies the flavor and natural sweetness of colorful
Oriental eggplants and red bell peppers.

◆

PER SERVING: *91 calories, 3 g protein, 17 g carbohydrates, 2 g total fat, 0 mg cholesterol, 10 mg sodium*

PREPARATION TIME: *20 min.*
GRILLING TIME: *15 min.*

5 or 6 Oriental eggplants
2 medium-size red bell
  peppers
3 large heads garlic
3 tsp. olive oil
3 Tbsp. balsamic vinegar
2 Tbsp. chopped parsley
Salt and pepper

Trim stems from eggplants. Cut eggplants in half lengthwise, turn cut side down; cut each piece lengthwise into thirds. Rinse bell peppers; stem, seed, and cut into strips or chunks. Set aside.

In a 5- to 6-quart pan, bring 3 quarts water to a boil over high heat. Add garlic, heads unpeeled, and cook, uncovered, for 10 minutes. Drain and cool slightly. Peel garlic.

Rub eggplants, bell peppers, and garlic very lightly with olive oil. Place in a mesh grill or basket and grill 4 to 6 inches above a solid bed of medium coals. Turn vegetables frequently until they are hot, tender, and streaked with brown (12 to 15 minutes).

Remove from grill, toss gently with balsamic vinegar, and sprinkle with parsley. Add salt and pepper to taste.

Makes about 4 servings

Grilled Pepper Gazpacho

*Grilled vegetables, blended
with chicken broth and lime juice, make
a cool soup for a summer party.*

◆

PER SERVING: *76 calories, 3 g protein, 16 g carbohydrates, 1 g total fat, 0 mg cholesterol, 382 mg sodium*

PREPARATION TIME: *10 min.*
GRILLING TIME: *10 min.*

3 *medium-size red bell
    peppers*
1½ *cups chicken broth*
¼ *cup lime juice*
3 *green onions (ends
    trimmed), finely chopped*
3 *medium-size Roma-type
    tomatoes, cored, diced*
2 *small bell peppers, yellow
    and green or 2 of one
    color, stemmed, seeded,
    diced*
Salt and pepper

Place whole red peppers on a grill 4 to 6 inches above a solid bed of medium coals. Cook, turning frequently, until peppers are streaked with brown and tender when pierced (8 to 10 minutes). Cool. Pull off any blackened skin; remove stems and seeds.

In a food processor or blender, smoothly purée peppers with broth and lime juice. Transfer to bowl and stir in onions, tomatoes, yellow and green bell peppers, and salt and pepper to taste.

Cover soup and refrigerate until cold, at least 2 hours or up to a day. Stir well before serving.

Makes 4 servings

Fennel, Potato & Green Bean Salad

*Tender green beans and
grilled fennel, coated with a sherry sauce,
dress up potato salad.*

◆

PER SERVING: *344 calories, 8 g protein, 45 g carbohydrates, 15 g total fat, 0 mg cholesterol, 179 mg sodium*

PREPARATION TIME: *25 min.*
GRILLING TIME: *30 min.*

1 *lb. green beans*
2 *large heads fennel, leaves,
   stalks, bulb base removed,
   heads cut into quarters
   lengthwise*
¼ *cup salad oil*
2 *large russet potatoes,
   peeled, cut into quarters
   lengthwise*
1 *tsp. each mustard seed,
   cumin seed, and fennel
   seed*
⅓ *cup sherry vinegar*
⅓ *cup Gewürztraminer
   or orange juice*
1 *Tbsp. grated lemon zest*
Salt and pepper

In a 5- to 6-quart pan, bring 8 cups water to a boil over high heat. Add beans and cook, uncovered, just until tender (about 6 minutes); drain.

Brush fennel with oil and place on a lightly greased grill 4 to 6 inches above a solid bed of medium coals. Cook, turning occasionally and brushing with oil, until browned and tender (about 20 minutes).

Place potatoes in a 5- to 6-quart pan; cover with water. Bring to a boil; reduce heat, cover, and boil gently until tender (about 6 minutes). Drain; brush with oil, and place on grill above medium coals. Cook, turning occasionally and brushing with oil, until browned (about 8 minutes).

In a small frying pan, stir mustard, cumin, and fennel seeds over medium heat until fragrant (about 2 minutes). Transfer to a nonreactive bowl, and combine with vinegar, Gewürztraminer, and lemon zest. On 4 plates, divide beans; top with potatoes, fennel, and dressing. Add salt and pepper to taste.

Makes 4 servings

Grilled Pepper
& Black Bean Salad

A cilantro and honey dressing
complements the flavors of grilled red bell
peppers and black beans.

◆

PER SERVING: *245 calories, 8 g protein, 31 g carbohydrates, 11 g total fat, 0 mg cholesterol, 741 mg sodium*

PREPARATION TIME: *15 min.*
GRILLING TIME: *10 min.*

2 *medium-size red bell
    peppers, cut in half
    lengthwise*
½ cup seasoned rice vinegar
¼ cup olive oil
1 Tbsp. honey
½ tsp. chili oil
¼ cup minced cilantro
*2 Tbsp. chopped green
    onion*
*3 cans (15 oz. each) black
    beans, drained, rinsed*
Cilantro sprigs
Salt and pepper

Place red peppers on a grill 4 to 6 inches above a solid bed of medium coals. Cook, turning frequently, until peppers are streaked with brown and tender when pierced (8 to 10 minutes). Cool. Pull off any blackened skin. Remove stem and seeds. Save juices. Cut into strips or chunks.

Meanwhile, in a nonreactive bowl, mix together rice vinegar, olive oil, honey, chili oil, minced cilantro, and green onion. Mix beans with cilantro dressing and roasted peppers and their juices. Pour into a serving bowl; garnish with cilantro sprigs. Season to taste with salt and pepper.

Makes about 6 servings

Broccoli &
Grilled Garlic Salad

*Mild-flavored roasted garlic,
soy sauce, and sesame oil add gusto to this
summertime broccoli salad.*

◆

PER SERVING: *155 calories, 7 g protein, 23 g carbohydrates, 6 g total fat, 0 mg cholesterol, 376 mg sodium*

PREPARATION TIME: *20 min.*
GRILLING TIME: *30 min.*

9 *cups broccoli flowerets*
3 *large heads garlic,
    separated into cloves*
2 *Tbsp. olive oil*
2 *Tbsp. soy sauce*
1 *tsp. sesame oil*

In a 5- to 6-quart pan, bring 3 to 4 quarts water to a boil over high heat. Add broccoli and cook just until tender (about 5 minutes). Drain, immerse in cold water until cool, and drain again. Pat dry.

In a 5- to 6-quart pan, bring 3 quarts water to a boil over high heat. Add unpeeled garlic cloves and cook, uncovered, for 10 minutes. Drain and let cool slightly. Peel garlic and thread cloves on metal skewers. Brush garlic with some of the olive oil and place on a lightly greased grill 4 to 6 inches above a solid bed of medium coals. Cook, turning frequently and brushing with more olive oil, until garlic is well browned and tender (about 20 minutes). Let cool and remove from skewers.

In a shallow bowl, mix soy sauce and sesame oil. Add broccoli and garlic cloves and mix lightly.

Makes 6 servings

Grilled Asparagus
& Shallot Salad

*Lightly grilled asparagus and sweet,
golden shallots team up with mixed greens
for an elegant salad.*

◆

PER SERVING: *263 calories, 8 g protein, 38 g carbohydrates, 11 g total fat, 0 mg cholesterol, 184 mg sodium*

PREPARATION TIME: *15 min.*
GRILLING TIME: *20 min.*

3 Tbsp. extra-virgin olive
   oil or salad oil
2 cloves garlic, minced
   or pressed
1 to 1¼ lb. asparagus,
   tough ends trimmed
1¾ lb. shallots, peeled
¾ cup beef broth
¼ cup balsamic or red
   wine vinegar
⅓ lb. (about 8 cups) bite-
   size pieces mixed salad
   greens or mesclun,
   rinsed, crisped
Salt and pepper

In a nonreactive bowl, mix oil and garlic. With a vegetable peeler, pare stems of asparagus. Brush asparagus with half the oil mixture, then set aside.

Thread shallots on 3 or 4 metal skewers. Brush with remaining oil mixture. Place skewers on a grill 6 inches above a solid bed of medium-hot coals. Cook, turning often, until shallots are well browned and tender when pierced (about 15 minutes).

Reserve 12 shallots. Trim scorched bits from remaining shallots and put them in a blender with broth and vinegar. Whirl until smooth; set aside.

Grill asparagus spears over medium coals, turning frequently, until lightly browned and just tender when pierced, 5 to 7 minutes; keep warm.

Mix ½ of the dressing with salad greens; divide among 4 dinner plates. Set asparagus beside salad, fanning spears. Garnish with reserved shallots. Serve with remaining dressing. Add salt and pepper to taste.

Makes 4 servings

Barley, Grilled Corn & Onion Salad

Grilled corn kernels and onions combine with cooked barley to make a great accompaniment to any grilled dish.

◆

PER SERVING: 222 calories, 8 g protein, 47 g carbohydrates, 2 g total fat, 0 mg cholesterol, 516 mg sodium

PREPARATION TIME: *45 min.*
GRILLING TIME: *15 min.*

4½ cups chicken broth
1½ cups pearl barley
1 Tbsp. grated lemon zest
4 large ears (10 to 12 inches long) yellow corn, husks, silk removed
2 large red onions, halved
2 cups lightly packed fresh mint, minced
½ cup minced cilantro
½ cup rice vinegar
½ tsp. pepper
Mint and cilantro sprigs
Salt

Combine broth, barley, and lemon zest in a 3- to 4-quart pan. Cover and bring to a boil over high heat; simmer until barley is tender to bite (about 30 minutes). Drain barley, reserving broth. If making ahead, cover and refrigerate barley and broth separately up to 1 day.

Barbecue corn and onions by indirect heat (see page 8), placing them on a grill 4 to 6 inches above hot coals. Cover barbecue with lid; if lid has vents, open them. Turn vegetables often until slightly charred (12 to 15 minutes); set aside until cool.

Cut corn from cobs and chop onions. In a non-reactive bowl, mix vegetables with barley, minced mint and cilantro, vinegar, pepper, and enough of the reserved broth to give salad the moistness you desire. Garnish with mint and cilantro sprigs; add salt to taste.

Makes 8 to 10 servings

Grilled Red Pepper Dip

The smoky-sweet taste of grilled red peppers permeates this yogurt-based dipping sauce.

◆

PER TABLESPOON: *13 calories, .36 g protein, 1 g carbohydrates, 1 g total fat, 1 mg cholesterol, 18 mg sodium*

PREPARATION TIME: *10 min.*
GRILLING TIME: *10 min.*

1 *large red bell pepper*
1 *clove garlic*
¼ *cup plain nonfat yogurt*
3 *Tbsp. reduced-calorie*
  mayonnaise
Salt

Place red peppers on a grill 4 to 6 inches above a solid bed of medium coals. Cook, turning frequently, until peppers are streaked with brown and tender when pierced (8 to 10 minutes). Cool. Pull off any blackened skin; remove stem and seeds.

In a blender or food processor, purée bell pepper, garlic, yogurt, and mayonnaise. Add salt to taste. If making ahead, cover and refrigerate up to a day.

Makes about 1 cup

KEBABS

Whether you're entertaining friends or treating the family, tempt them with vegetable kebabs sizzling hot off the grill. The recipes that follow range from marinated artichoke kebabs that give grilled fish and chicken a special flair to grilled banana squash enlivened by a bold cranberry salsa.

HERB-MARINATED KEBABS, RECIPE ON PAGE 30

Herb-marinated Kebabs

(PICTURED ON PAGE 28)

*Even the confirmed meat-and-potato buff will find these herb-marinated grilled vegetables
hard to resist. Serve them with a green salad and crusty bread.*

◆

PER SERVING: *463 calories, 10 g protein, 62 g carbohydrates, 22 g total fat, 0 mg cholesterol, 66 mg sodium*

PREPARATION TIME: *1 hr.*
GRILLING TIME: *15 min.*

1 *small unpeeled eggplant*
2 *large carrots*
1 *dozen small thin-skinned
   potatoes*
¾ *cup salad oil*
¼ *cup white wine vinegar*
2 *cloves garlic, minced*
1 *tsp.* each *Dijon mustard,
   dry basil, and oregano*
½ *tsp.* each *fresh marjoram
   and dry rosemary*
¼ *tsp. pepper*
3 *medium-size zucchini, cut
   crosswise into 1-inch slices*
2 *small red or green bell
   peppers, seeded, cut into
   1-inch squares*
1 *large onion, cut in wedges,
   layers separated*
16 *whole large mushrooms*
Salt

Cut eggplant into 2-inch cubes; cook in 1 inch of boiling water for 3 minutes; drain. Cut carrots into ½-inch slices; cook in 1 inch of boiling water until crisp-tender (about 6 minutes); drain. Cook unpeeled potatoes in 1 inch of boiling water until tender (about 20 minutes); drain and cut in half.

In a nonreactive bowl, combine oil, vinegar, garlic, mustard, basil, oregano, marjoram, rosemary, and pepper.

Place eggplant, carrots, potatoes, zucchini, bell peppers, onion, and mushrooms in a plastic bag. Pour marinade over vegetables. Seal bag and refrigerate for 2 hours or until next day.

Drain and reserve marinade from vegetables. Onto 8 sturdy metal skewers, alternately thread vegetables. Place on a lightly greased grill 4 to 6 inches above a solid bed of low-glowing coals. Cook, turning and basting with reserved marinade until vegetables are tender (10 to 15 minutes). Add salt to taste.

Makes 4 servings

Sweet Potatoes with Lime & Tequila

*Lime and tequila bring
the vibrant flavors of Mexico to sweet
potatoes hot off the grill.*

◆

PER SERVING: *216 calories, 3 g protein, 50 g carbohydrates, .52 g total fat, 0 mg cholesterol, 24 mg sodium*

PREPARATION TIME: *15 min.*
GRILLING TIME: *8 min.*

2 *lb. sweet potatoes*
¼ *cup lime juice*
2 *Tbsp. honey*
1 *Tbsp. tequila*

Peel sweet potatoes and cut crosswise into ¾-inch-thick slices. In a 5- to 6-quart pan, bring 3 quarts water to a boil over high heat. Add potatoes and cook just until tender (about 6 minutes); drain.

In a small nonreactive bowl, mix lime juice, honey, and tequila. Brush potatoes with some of the lime juice mixture and place on a lightly greased grill 4 to 6 inches above a solid bed of medium coals. Cook, turning frequently and brushing with remaining juice mixture, until potatoes are browned (about 8 minutes).

Makes 4 servings

Artichoke Kebabs

*Tiny marinated artichokes
are trimmed before skewering and grilling,
so you can enjoy every morsel.*

◆

PER SERVING: 88 calories, 3 g protein, 9 g carbohydrates, 6 g total fat, 0 mg cholesterol, 78 mg sodium

PREPARATION TIME: *15 min.*
GRILLING TIME: *15 min.*

2 *Tbsp. lemon juice*
2 *Tbsp. olive oil*
1 *tsp. minced fresh thyme
   or ½ tsp. dried thyme*
18 *small (1½- to 2-inches-
   wide) artichokes*
Salt and pepper

In a nonreactive bowl, combine lemon juice, oil, thyme, and 2 tablespoons water.

Trim stems flush with artichoke bottoms. Break off leaves down to pale, tender ones. Cut off the top ⅓ to ½ of each artichoke to remove thorny tips. With a small, sharp knife, smoothly trim fibrous portions from bottoms. If trimmed artichokes are wider than 1½ inches, cut in half lengthwise. As trimmed, coat in lemon marinade. Thread hearts onto metal flat-blade skewers; reserve remaining marinade.

Place artichokes on a grill 4 to 6 inches above a solid bed of medium-hot coals. Turn often until artichoke bottoms are tender when pierced, and artichokes are lightly browned all over (12 to 15 minutes). Place skewered artichokes on a platter; drizzle with remaining marinade. Add salt and pepper to taste.

Makes 4 to 6 servings

Sake Kasu on Vegetables

*Although new to the Western palate, sake lees
(the residue of rice wine production) has been used in Japan
for centuries to preserve food.*

◆

*PER SERVING: 275 calories, 44 g protein, 12 g carbohydrates, 5 g total fat, 93 mg cholesterol, 818 mg sodium

PREPARATION TIME: *25 min.*
GRILLING TIME: *10 min.*

*½ lb. sake lees, paste or
sheets (available in
Asian markets)*
*6 Tbsp. each mirin
and water*
2 Tbsp. sugar
*3 medium-size red bell
peppers, stemmed,
seeded, cut into 8 equal-
size wedges*
*9 small yellow or green
pattypan squash*

*Does not include marinade

In a blender or food processor, whirl together sake lees, mirin, water, and sugar until smooth. Cover and refrigerate until ready to use, up to 1 week.

Meanwhile, in a 3- to 4-quart pan, bring about 2 quarts water to a boil over high heat. Add pepper wedges and cook just until tender (about 3 minutes). Lift from water with a slotted spoon; set aside. Add squash and cook until tender when pierced with a fork (about 6 minutes); drain, cool, and cut in halves. If made ahead, cover and refrigerate up to 1 day.

In a nonreactive bowl, mix pepper and squash with 1 cup sake lees marinade. Using two-prong skewers, alternately thread 4 pepper wedges and 3 squash halves. Place skewers on a grill 4 to 6 inches above a solid bed of medium coals, grilling until browned (about 5 minutes on each side).

Makes 6 servings

Banana Squash with Cranberry Salsa

*An ideal addition to
a holiday barbecue buffet, these kebabs are served
with a dollop of cranberry salsa.*

◆

PER SERVING: *180 calories, 2 g protein, 15 g carbohydrates, 14 g total fat, 0 mg cholesterol, 5 mg sodium*

PREPARATION TIME: *20 min.*
GRILLING TIME: *30 min.*

½ cup olive oil
2 garlic cloves, minced
   or pressed
1½ cups fresh or frozen
   cranberries
½ small onion
¼ cup firmly packed parsley
½ tsp. crushed dried hot
   red chiles
1 tsp. each grated orange
   zest and lemon juice
2 Tbsp. orange juice
1½ Tbsp. honey
1½ lb. seeded banana
   squash, cut into about
   1½- by 4-inch rectangles

Combine olive oil and garlic, cover, and refrigerate up to 4 hours.

In a food processor, or with a large knife, finely chop cranberries, onion, parsley, and chiles. Mix with the orange zest, lemon juice, orange juice, and honey. If made ahead, put in a covered container and refrigerate up to 2 days.

Thread 4 or 5 pieces of squash, perpendicular to wide sides, onto a 10- to 12-inch metal skewer. Thread another skewer through squash, parallel to the first and about 1½ inches from it. Repeat the procedure with the remaining squash.

On a barbecue with a lid, place grill 4 to 6 inches above a solid layer of medium coals. Lay skewered squash on grill and baste with garlic oil. Cover and cook, turning and basting every 10 minutes, until squash is tender when pierced (about 30 minutes). Remove squash from skewers onto a platter; serve with the cranberry salsa.

Makes 8 servings

Eggplant & Shiitake Kebabs

*After soaking in a honey-soy
marinade, vegetables and tofu are grilled to
an evenly browned perfection.*

◆

PER SERVING: *243 calories, 13 g protein, 32 g carbohydrates, 10 g total fat, 0 mg cholesterol, 788 mg sodium*

PREPARATION TIME: *15 min.*
GRILLING TIME: *12 min.*

1 *Tbsp. sesame oil*
3 *Tbsp. soy sauce*
2 *Tbsp. honey*
1 *tsp. chili oil*
16 *medium-size fresh
    shiitake mushrooms,
    stems removed*
½ *lb. firm tofu, cut
    into 8 cubes*
2 *Japanese eggplants, cut
    crosswise into 1-inch-
    thick slices*
1 *large yellow bell pepper,
    seeded, cut into 1½-inch
    squares*
8 *cherry tomatoes*

In a deep, nonreactive bowl, mix sesame oil, soy sauce, honey, and chili oil. Add mushrooms and tofu and turn to coat. Cover and refrigerate for 30 minutes, turning occasionally.

Carefully lift mushrooms and tofu out of marinade; add eggplants, bell pepper, and cherry tomatoes to marinade; turn to coat, then lift out vegetables, and reserve marinade. On 4 sturdy metal skewers, thread eggplants, bell pepper, and tomatoes alternately with mushrooms and tofu.

Place skewers on a lightly greased grill 4 to 6 inches above a solid bed of medium coals. Cook, turning and basting frequently with remaining marinade, until vegetables are well browned and eggplant is tender (about 12 minutes).

Makes 4 servings

STUFFED VEGETABLES

*C*hiles, zucchini, and bell peppers have added appeal when stuffed with savory fillings. In the pages that follow, you'll find recipes with a definite Mexican flavor and others with a hint of Italy. Whichever you choose, remember that you can mix and match the fillings with the vegetables.

Chiles with Eggs & Lime Salsa

(PICTURED ON PAGE 38)

*Fat content is kept to a minimum when poblano chiles
are grilled rather than fried prior to stuffing.*

◆

PER SERVING: 174 calories, 16 g protein, 22 g carbohydrates, 3 g total fat, 110 mg cholesterol, 858 mg sodium

PREPARATION TIME: *15 min.*
GRILLING TIME: *10 min.*

1 *large ripe red or yellow
   tomato*
8 *medium-size tomatillos*
¼ *cup minced red or yellow
   bell pepper*
2 *Tbsp. minced red onion*
1 *tsp. grated lime zest*
1 *Tbsp. lime juice*
4 *fresh green poblano chiles*
2 *large eggs*
4 *large egg whites*
½ *cup each nonfat cottage
   cheese and finely chopped
   spinach leaves*
⅓ *cup sliced green onion*
2 *tsp. cornstarch blended
   with 1 Tbsp. cold water*
1½ *tsp. fresh thyme*
⅛ *tsp. each salt and white
   pepper*

Finely dice tomato. Husk, rinse, and chop tomatillos. Mix tomato, tomatillos, bell pepper, onion, lime zest, and lime juice. Cover and refrigerate up to 4 hours.

Rinse chiles and pat dry. Place on a grill 4 to 6 inches above a solid bed of medium coals. Grill for 8 to 10 minutes. Cool. Pull off any blackened skin. Slit 1 side of each chile almost, but not all the way, to stem end and tip; do not puncture chile elsewhere. Discard seeds and veins.

In a food processor, smoothly purée eggs, egg whites, cottage cheese, spinach, 1 tablespoon onion, cornstarch mixture, thyme, salt, and pepper.

Heat oil in a medium-size nonstick frying pan over medium heat. Add egg mixture to pan; stir often until softly scrambled (3 to 5 minutes).

Spoon mixture equally into chiles. Set on a platter; serve with lime salsa.

Makes 4 servings

Bell Peppers Stuffed with Corn

*Carefully trimmed
red bell peppers make attractive containers
for cheese-topped corn kernels.*

◆

PER SERVING: *300 calories, 12 g protein, 31 g carbohydrates, 16 g total fat, 45 mg cholesterol, 251 mg sodium*

PREPARATION TIME: *15 min.*
GRILLING TIME: *10 min.*

5 medium-size red bell
   peppers
1 large onion
2 Tbsp. butter
2 cups fresh or frozen
   corn kernels
1 cup shredded sharp
   Cheddar cheese

Cut off stem ends of peppers and remove seeds. Chop 1 pepper and onion.

Melt butter in a large frying pan over medium-high heat. Add chopped pepper and onion, and cook, stirring often, until onion is soft (about 10 minutes). Add corn kernels to pan and cook, stirring, until corn is hot.

Transfer corn mixture to a bowl. Add cheese and mix lightly. Fill peppers equally with corn mixture.

Set peppers, filling side up, on a lightly greased grill 4 to 6 inches above a solid bed of medium coals. Cover barbecue, open vents, and cook until pepper shells are soft and cheese is melted (about 10 minutes).

Makes 4 servings

Savory Chiles Relleños

*Lean and simple
to make, these grilled chiles retain
their pronounced flavor.*

◆

PER SERVING: *169 calories, 6 g protein, 18 g carbohydrates, 9 g total fat, 27 mg cholesterol, 210 mg sodium*

PREPARATION TIME: *35 min.*
GRILLING TIME: *15 min.*

1 large tomato, coarsely
   chopped
¼ cup chopped onion
1 to 1½ Tbsp. *finely chopped
   seeded fresh or canned
   jalapeño chiles*
1 Tbsp. each *chopped
   cilantro and white wine
   vinegar*
1 clove garlic, minced
   or pressed
8 to 12 large Anaheim chiles
3 Tbsp. butter
3 large onions, thinly sliced
½ cup golden raisins
3 to 4 Tbsp. minced
   drained, seeded canned
   chipotle chiles in sauce
1½ cups shredded
   jack cheese

In a nonreactive bowl, stir together tomato, chopped onion, jalapeño chiles, cilantro, vinegar, and garlic. Cover and refrigerate for at least 2 hours or until next day.

Place Anaheim chiles on a lightly greased grill 4 to 6 inches above a solid bed of hot coals. Cook, uncovered, without turning, until chiles are blistered and slightly charred on one side (2 to 3 minutes). Remove from grill, peel off any blistered skin, and slit each chile lengthwise down cooked side. Scrape out seeds but leave chiles whole.

Melt butter in a wide frying pan over medium heat. Add sliced onions; cook, stirring often, until onions are light gold (about 15 minutes). Stir in raisins and chipotle chiles. Let cool. Then stir in jack cheese.

Evenly fill chiles with onion mixture. Place chiles, slit side up, on grill 4 to 6 inches above a solid bed of medium coals. Cover barbecue, cook until onion mixture is hot to touch (7 to 10 minutes). Serve with salsa.

Makes about 8 servings

Grilled Tomato-topped Polenta

*Golden brown polenta slices,
topped with mozzarella cheese, tomatoes, and basil,
evoke the tastes of Italy.*

◆

PER SERVING: 354 calories, 13 g protein, 25 g carbohydrates, 23 g total fat, 27 mg cholesterol, 782 mg sodium

PREPARATION TIME: *45 min.*
GRILLING TIME: *15 min.*

4½ cups chicken broth
1½ cups polenta
*4 large firm-ripe tomatoes
(each about 4 inches in
diameter), tops and
bottoms trimmed, cut
in half crosswise*
½ cup basil oil
*8 oz. smoked mozzarella
cheese, cut into 8 slices*
*½ cup grated Parmesan
cheese*
8 large fresh basil leaves

In a 4- to 5-quart pan, bring broth to a boil over
high heat. Pour polenta in a thin stream into boiling
broth. Cook, stirring with a wooden spoon, until
thickened (about 5 minutes). Reduce heat to low;
cook, stirring, for 10 more minutes. Immediately
pour polenta into a well-greased 4- by 8-inch loaf
pan; let cool until firm (about 30 minutes).

Run a knife around edges of pan and turn polenta
out onto a board. Carefully cut crosswise into 8 slices.

Brush polenta slices and tomato halves generously
with the oil. Place tomatoes on lightly greased grill 4
to 6 inches above a solid bed of medium coals. Cook,
turning once, until tomatoes are browned (about 8
minutes). Meanwhile, add polenta to grill and cook,
turning once, until slices are browned (about 4 minutes). Transfer polenta to serving plate. Top each
polenta slice with a slice of mozzarella, then with a
tomato. Sprinkle with Parmesan and top with basil.

Makes 8 servings

Chiles Relleños with Shrimp

*Stuffed with shrimp and served
with salsa, grilled chiles can be served as
a side dish or light entrée.*

◆

PER SERVING: *64 calories, 10 g protein, 5 g carbohydrates, .59 g total fat, 89 mg cholesterol, 106 mg sodium*

PREPARATION TIME: *15 min.*
GRILLING TIME: *10 min.*

1 large tomato, chopped
¼ cup chopped onion
*1 to 1½ Tbsp. finely chopped
seeded fresh or canned
jalapeño or drained,
seeded canned chipotle
chiles in sauce*
*1 Tbsp. each chopped
cilantro and white wine
vinegar*
*1 clove garlic, minced
or pressed*
*8 to 12 large (each 6 to 6½
inches long) mild green
chiles such as Anaheim*
1 lb. small cooked shrimp
¾ cup sliced green onions
Sour cream

In a nonreactive bowl, stir together tomato, onion, jalapeño, cilantro, vinegar, and garlic. Cover and refrigerate for at least 2 hours or until next day.

Place chiles on a lightly greased grill 4 to 6 inches above a solid bed of hot coals. Cook, uncovered, without turning, until chiles are blistered and slightly charred on one side (2 to 3 minutes). Remove from grill; peel off any blistered skin that comes off easily. Slit each chile lengthwise down cooked side. Scrape out seeds but leave chiles whole.

Mix shrimp and onions; fill chiles equally. Place chiles, slit side up, on grill 4 to 6 inches above a solid bed of medium coals. Cover barbecue. Cook until shrimp mixture is hot to touch (5 to 7 minutes). Transfer chiles to plates; serve with salsa and sour cream.

Makes 4 servings

Grilled Stuffed Zucchini

A rice and zucchini mixture,
topped with melted cheese, fits neatly into
hollowed-out zucchini shells.

◆

PER SERVING: *189 calories, 8 g protein, 18 g carbohydrates, 10 g total fat, 29 mg cholesterol, 107 mg sodium*

PREPARATION TIME: *25 min.*
GRILLING TIME: *10 min.*

4 *medium-size zucchini*
2 *Tbsp. butter*
6 *green onions, finely*
  chopped
1 *cup cooked brown rice*
½ *cup shredded Swiss*
  cheese

Trim and discard ends of zucchini; cut each in half lengthwise. With a small knife or spoon, scoop out centers, leaving a shell ¼ inch thick. Finely chop the flesh from the centers.

Melt butter in a medium-size frying pan over medium-high heat. With tongs, dip zucchini shells in butter, then set zucchini shells aside. Add chopped zucchini and onions to pan. Cook, stirring often, until zucchini is lightly browned (about 10 minutes).

Transfer zucchini mixture to a bowl. Add rice and ¼ cup cheese; mix lightly. Fill zucchini shells equally with rice mixture. Top with remaining cheese.

Set zucchini shells, filling side up, on a lightly greased grill 4 to 6 inches above a solid bed of medium coals. Cover barbecue, open vents, and cook until shells are soft and cheese is melted (about 10 minutes).

Makes 4 servings

Chorizo-stuffed Chiles

*Chorizo, a spicy Mexican-style sausage,
is seasoned with cumin and oregano to make
this piquant filling.*

◆

PER SERVING: 127 calories, 6 g protein, 8 g carbohydrates, 8 g total fat, 42 mg cholesterol, 242 mg sodium

PREPARATION TIME: *30 min.*
GRILLING TIME: *15 min.*

6 oz. chorizo sausage
1 clove garlic, minced
   or pressed
½ tsp. ground cumin
¼ tsp. dried oregano leaves
1 lb. fresh spinach,
   stemmed, chopped
¼ lb. mushrooms, finely
   chopped
1 cup soft bread crumbs
⅓ cup shredded jack cheese
1 egg, beaten
Salt
8 large fresh mild green
   chiles, such as Anaheim
   or poblano

Crumble sausage into a wide frying pan. Add garlic, cumin, and oregano. Cook over medium-high heat, stirring frequently, until meat is browned (about 10 minutes). Discard all but 2 tablespoons fat.

Add spinach and mushrooms to sausage and cook, stirring frequently, until liquid has evaporated (about 10 minutes). Remove from heat and stir in bread crumbs, cheese, and egg. Mix well; season to taste with salt. Set aside.

Place chiles on a lightly greased grill 4 to 6 inches above a solid bed of hot coals. Cook, uncovered, without turning, until chiles are blistered and slightly charred on one side (2 to 3 minutes). Remove from grill; peel off any blistered skin that comes off easily. Slit each chile lengthwise down cooked side. Scrape out seeds but leave chiles whole.

Fill chiles equally with sausage mixture. Return chiles to grill, slit side up. Cover barbecue and cook until mixture is hot to touch (5 to 7 minutes).

Makes 4 servings

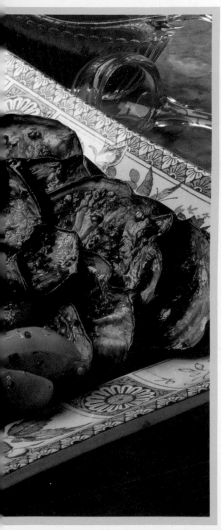

SIMPLE & DELICIOUS

All vegetables seem to

taste better hot off the grill.

Whether you are simply

grilling corn or preparing a

platter of mixed vegetables,

you can accentuate the

smoky flavors of these side

dishes by serving them with

an herb dressing, citrus salsa,

or sesame sauce.

RUSTIC GRILLED VEGETABLES, RECIPE ON PAGE 50

Rustic Grilled Vegetables

(PICTURED ON PAGE 48)

An herb-flavored dressing enhances
this colorful combination of grilled vegetables.

◆

PER SERVING: 252 calories, 3 g protein, 17 g carbohydrates, 20 g total fat, 0 mg cholesterol, 15 mg sodium

PREPARATION TIME: *15 min.*
GRILLING TIME: *10 min.*

¾ cup olive oil
⅔ cup balsamic or red
 wine vinegar
¼ cup chopped chives
 or green onion tops
2 tsp. chopped fresh oregano
 or 1 tsp. dried oregano
4 medium-size zucchini
3 small eggplants
2 each medium-size yellow
 and red bell peppers,
 seeded
3 large red onions
Salt and pepper

In a nonreactive bowl, combine ⅓ cup of the oil, ⅓ cup of the vinegar, the chives, and oregano. Cover and let stand for up to 4 hours; stir well before using.

Cut zucchini lengthwise into ⅓-inch-thick slices. Cut eggplants lengthwise into ½-inch-thick slices. Cut bell peppers lengthwise into sixths. Brush the vegetables lightly with some of the remaining oil.

Cut onions crosswise into ½-inch-thick slices. Brush generously with remaining vinegar, then brush lightly with some of the oil.

Place vegetables on a greased grill 4 to 6 inches above a solid bed of medium coals. Cook, turning often and brushing with more oil, until all are browned and tender (about 10 minutes). Let vegetables cool to room temperature, then arrange on a large platter, pour dressing over them, and season to taste with salt and pepper.

Makes 8 to 10 servings

Vegetables Provençal

*F*lavored vinegar adds zip
to this late-summer feast of grilled peppers,
squash, and onions.

◆

PER SERVING: *194 calories, 5 g protein, 27 g carbohydrates, 9 g total fat, 3 mg cholesterol, 85 mg sodium*

PREPARATION TIME: *20 min.*
GRILLING TIME: *15 min.*

¾ lb. 2-inch-diameter
thin-skinned potatoes
2 large red bell peppers
6 medium-size yellow or
green pattypan squash
2 medium-size onions
3 Tbsp. extra-virgin
olive oil
¼ cup finely shredded
Parmesan cheese
¼ cup shredded fresh basil
Fresh basil sprigs
½ cup herb, onion, or
garlic vinegar
Salt and pepper

Halve potatoes. Place in a 2-quart pan; cover with water. Simmer, covered, until just tender when pierced (about 8 minutes); drain.

Stem and seed peppers; cut each lengthwise into sixths. Halve squash horizontally. Cut onions crosswise into ½-inch rounds. Divide all vegetables between 2 large bowls. Drizzle oil equally over each; mix to coat.

Place vegetables (one portion at a time, if necessary) on a greased grill over a solid bed of medium coals. Cook, turning often, until all are streaked brown (10 to 12 minutes).

Arrange on a platter. Scatter cheese and basil on top; garnish with basil sprigs. Pour vinegar on top; season with salt and pepper.

Makes 6 servings

Ratatouille-Cheese Sandwiches

*Italian bread slices, topped with lightly
grilled vegetables and melted cheese, make a tasty
and nutritious lunch dish.*

◆

PER SERVING: *594 calories, 24 g protein, 53 g carbohydrates, 33 g total fat, 66 mg cholesterol, 910 mg sodium*

PREPARATION TIME: *20 min.*
GRILLING TIME: *20 min.*

1 *medium-size eggplant,
   stem trimmed, cut into
   1-inch chunks*
2 *medium-size zucchini,
   ends trimmed, sliced*
2 *large red bell peppers,
   stemmed, seeded, cut into
   1½-inch pieces*
1 *clove garlic, minced
   or pressed*
⅓ *cup olive oil*
3 *Tbsp. lemon juice*
2 *Tbsp. chopped fresh basil*
1 *Tbsp. chopped fresh
   marjoram*
6 *medium-size Roma tomatoes, cut in half lengthwise*
1 *long loaf flat Italian bread*
3 *cups shredded fontina
   cheese*

Thread eggplant, zucchini, and pepper pieces onto
skewers. Combine garlic, oil, lemon juice, basil, and
marjoram. Lightly brush vegetables and tomatoes
with some of the oil mixture. Place skewers and tomatoes on a lightly greased grill over a solid bed of medium coals. Cook, turning frequently, until vegetables
are streaked with brown and tender when pierced;
(12 to 15 minutes for skewers; 8 to 12 minutes for
tomatoes). Transfer to a platter; remove skewers.

Meanwhile, cut bread diagonally into 3 equal
pieces, then split each piece horizontally. Brush cut
sides with remaining oil mixture. Place bread, cut
side down, on grill until toasted (about 3 minutes).
Remove from grill, top toasted sides equally with
cheese and vegetables.

Return bread to grill, cheese side up; cover barbecue, open vents, and cook until cheese melts (3 to 4
minutes); be careful not to scorch bottom of bread.

Makes 6 servings

Chili Eggplant & Corn

*Flavored vinegars add pizzazz
and almost no calories to this tender eggplant
and golden corn medley.*

◆

PER SERVING: *159 calories, 3 g protein, 16 g carbohydrates, 11 g total fat, 0 mg cholesterol, 16 mg sodium*

PREPARATION TIME: *10 min.*
GRILLING TIME: *15 min.*

6 *medium-size Asian
    eggplants*
2 *large ears yellow corn*
3 *Tbsp. extra-virgin
    olive oil*
½ *cup chili, onion, garlic,
    or lemongrass vinegar,
    or a combination*
2 *Tbsp. minced fresh
    parsley or cilantro*
Salt and pepper

Halve eggplants lengthwise from base to within ½ inch of stem; press pieces to flatten and spread apart. Remove husks and silk from corn; cut into 1- to 1½-inch rounds. Rub corn and the cut surfaces of eggplants with oil.

Place vegetables on a greased grill over a solid bed of medium-hot coals. Cook, turning often, until eggplants are tender when pressed (8 to 10 minutes) and corn is golden (10 to 12 minutes).

Lift to a platter. Pour half of vinegar on top. Sprinkle with parsley; add salt, pepper, and remaining vinegar to taste.

Makes 4 servings

Corn on the Grill

*Let the fresh flavor of cilantro
accent ears of sweet corn as they grill
atop the barbecue.*

◆

PER SERVING: *243 calories, 10 g protein, 18 g carbohydrates, 16 g total fat, 43 mg cholesterol, 586 mg sodium*

PREPARATION TIME: *15 min.*
GRILLING TIME: *20 min.*

6 *ears of corn*
¼ *cup butter or margarine,
    at room temperature*
½ *cup firmly packed
    cilantro, chopped*
Salt and pepper
1 *cup sour cream (optional)*
6 *oz. grated Parmesan
    cheese*

Gently peel back corn husks but do not tear off. Pull out and discard silk; rinse corn and pat dry.

Cut 6 rectangles of aluminum foil, each 8 inches wide. Rub butter over each cob and sprinkle with cilantro. Season to taste with salt and pepper. Pull husks back over corn and wrap each ear in foil.

Place corn on a grill 4 to 6 inches above a solid bed of medium-hot coals. Cook, turning 2 or 3 times, for 20 minutes. Remove corn and carefully peel off foil; let cool slightly. Peel back husks and spread each ear with sour cream, if desired; sprinkle with cheese.

Makes 6 servings

Grilled Potatoes with Basil

Served at room temperature,
grill-roasted potatoes are perked up with
lemon juice and fresh basil.

◆

PER SERVING: *149 calories, 2 g protein, 21 g carbohydrates, 6 g total fat, 0 mg cholesterol, 10 mg sodium*

PREPARATION TIME: *10 min.*
GRILLING TIME: *40 min.*

16 small (about 1½ inches
  wide) red thin-skinned
  potatoes, scrubbed
¼ cup extra-virgin olive oil
2 Tbsp. lemon juice
2 Tbsp. grated lemon zest
½ cup shredded fresh basil
Basil sprigs (optional)
Salt and pepper

Cut potatoes in half crosswise and rub lightly with oil. Place cut side down on a lightly greased grill 4 to 6 inches above a solid bed of hot coals. Cover grill with lid; open vents. Turn potatoes occasionally until browned and tender when pierced (30 to 40 minutes).

In a bowl, mix potatoes with remaining oil, lemon juice, and lemon zest. Let stand until room temperature. Just before serving, stir in shredded basil and garnish with basil sprigs. Season to taste with salt and pepper.

Makes 8 to 10 servings

Potatoes & Carrots in Citrus Sauce

Richly browned potatoes and
carrots are tossed with a light citrus-chile dressing
for a zesty Mexican touch.

◆

PER SERVING: 191 calories, 3 g protein, 36 g carbohydrates, 4 g total fat, 0 mg cholesterol, 77 mg sodium

PREPARATION TIME: *20 min.*
GRILLING TIME: *10 min.*

2 lb. small (about 1½ inches
  wide) red thin-skinned
  potatoes
12 small carrots
2 Tbsp. olive oil or salad oil
2 tsp. grated orange zest
½ cup orange juice
2 Tbsp. white wine vinegar
2 Tbsp. minced fresh basil
  or 2 tsp. dry basil
1 fresh jalapeño chile,
  seeded, minced
1 Tbsp. honey
2 tsp. Dijon mustard
1 tsp. ground cumin
2 cloves garlic, pressed
Salt and pepper

Cut potatoes in half and place in a 5- to 6-quart
pan; add water to cover. Bring to a boil; reduce heat,
cover, and boil gently until tender when pierced
(about 6 minutes); drain.

In a 5- to 6-quart pan, bring 8 cups of water to
a boil over high heat. Add carrots and cook just
until tender (about 6 minutes); drain.

Brush potatoes and carrots lightly with some of
the oil. Place on a lightly greased grill 4 to 6 inches
above a bed of medium coals. Cook, turning occasionally and brushing with more oil, until vegetables
are browned (about 8 minutes). Cut carrots crosswise into thirds.

In a nonreactive bowl, combine orange zest,
orange juice, vinegar, basil, jalapeño chile, honey,
mustard, cumin, and garlic.

In a shallow bowl, combine potatoes, carrots,
and citrus sauce. Serve hot or warm. Before
serving, season to taste with salt and pepper.

Makes 6 servings

Grilled Vegetables on Cornbread

__B__ake cornbread in an 8-inch-square pan,
using your favorite recipe or mix, then top the bread with
dried tomatoes, olives, and eggplant.

◆

PER SERVING: 455 calories, 17 g protein, 17 g carbohydrates, 37 g total fat, 66 mg cholesterol, 621 mg sodium

PREPARATION TIME: *20 min.*
GRILLING TIME: *20 min.*

4 *small leeks*
1 *small eggplant*
4 *Tbsp. olive oil*
2 *Tbsp. balsamic or red*
  wine vinegar
2 *Tbsp. each drained,*
  minced dried tomatoes
  packed in oil and Greek-
  style olives
1 *Tbsp. minced fresh or 1*
  tsp. dry rosemary
1 *clove garlic, minced*
Prepared cornbread
½ *lb. fontina cheese,*
  shredded

Trim and discard root and tough stems of leeks; cut in half lengthwise, rinse well, and drain. Cut off eggplant stem, then cut eggplant lengthwise in 8 wedges.

Brush vegetables with 1 tablespoon of the oil and place on a grill 4 to 6 inches above a bed of medium coals. Turn often until vegetables brown and eggplant is very soft when pressed (8 to 10 minutes for leeks; 15 to 20 minutes for eggplant). If made ahead, let stand up to 6 hours.

Meanwhile, in a nonreactive bowl, combine vinegar, remaining olive oil, dried tomatoes, olives, rosemary, and garlic; mix well.

Cut prepared cornbread into 4 equal triangles and split horizontally. Lay bread, cut side up, on a 12- by 15-inch baking sheet. Arrange leeks and eggplant equally on bread; top equally with dried tomato relish and cheese. Broil 6 inches from heat until cheese melts (3 to 4 minutes). With a wide spatula, place 2 triangles on each of 4 dinner plates.

Does not include cornbread

Makes 4 servings

Toasted Sesame Squash
& Shiitake

*Grilled marinated vegetables,
soaked in a spicy toasted sesame sauce, make ideal
companions to a patio meal.*

◆

PER SERVING: *309 calories, 6 g protein, 24 g carbohydrates, 21 g total fat, 0 mg cholesterol, 784 mg sodium*

PREPARATION TIME: *10 min.*
GRILLING TIME: *15 min.*

*½ cup sesame seeds
3 Tbsp. salad oil
¼ cup water
2 Tbsp. lemon juice
2 Tbsp. minced fresh ginger
3 Tbsp. soy sauce
1 Tbsp. sugar
1 clove garlic
⅛ tsp. ground red pepper
  (cayenne)
¼ cup dry sherry or sake
½ Tbsp. Oriental sesame oil
8 green onions, ends
  trimmed
4 small crookneck squash,
  cut in half lengthwise
8 large fresh or soaked dry
  shiitake mushrooms,
  stems removed*

In an 8- to 10-inch frying pan, cook sesame seeds over medium-low heat, shaking pan often, until golden (10 to 12 minutes). In a blender, whirl hot sesame seeds and salad oil until a fine paste forms. Add water, lemon juice, ginger, 2 tablespoons soy sauce, sugar, garlic, and ground red pepper. Whirl until smooth. If made ahead, cover and refrigerate up to 2 days.

Combine sherry, 1 tablespoon soy sauce, and sesame oil; mix with vegetables. If made ahead, cover and refrigerate up to 2 hours.

Place vegetables on a grill 4 to 6 inches above a solid bed of medium-hot coals. Brush vegetables occasionally with remaining marinade and turn as needed to brown evenly. Cook until onions and mushrooms are lightly browned and squash is tender when pierced. Remove from grill as done and keep warm; serve with sesame sauce.

Makes 4 servings

Vegetables with Fresh Herbs

*For added flavor, brush bell peppers,
onions, summer squash, and leeks with olive oil and
fresh herbs before grilling them.*

◆

PER SERVING: 206 calories, 2 g protein, 16 g carbohydrates, 16 g total fat, 0 mg cholesterol, 9 mg sodium

PREPARATION TIME: *20 min.*
GRILLING TIME: *15 min.*

2 *red or yellow onions*
2 *crookneck squash,
    pattypan squash, or
    zucchini*
2 *slender leeks*
2 *red, yellow, or green
    bell peppers*
½ *cup olive oil or salad oil*
2 *Tbsp. minced fresh herbs,
    such as oregano, thyme,
    rosemary, tarragon, or a
    combination; or 2 tsp.
    dry herbs*
Salt and pepper

Peel onions and cut in half lengthwise. Trim ends from squash and cut in half lengthwise. Trim and discard root ends and any tough or wilted leaves from leeks; split leeks in half lengthwise and rinse well. Leave bell peppers whole (or cut in half, if large).

In a 4- to 6-quart pan, bring 2 quarts water to a boil over high heat. Add squash and leeks and boil for 2 minutes; drain, plunge into ice water, and drain again.

In a small bowl, stir together oil and herbs. Brush vegetables with oil mixture, then place on a greased grill 4 to 6 inches above a solid bed of hot coals. Cook, turning and basting often with remaining oil mixture, until vegetables are tender and streaked with brown (6 to 8 minutes for squash and leeks; 10 to 15 minutes for onions and peppers). Season to taste with salt and pepper.

Makes 6 servings

Garden Bounty

A cornucopia of fresh garden vegetables
surrounds a platter of wild and long-grain brown rice
for a hearty summer salad.

♦

PER SERVING: *518 calories, 14 g protein, 88 g carbohydrates, 16 g total fat, 0 mg cholesterol, 48 mg sodium*

PREPARATION TIME: *20 min.*
GRILLING TIME: *15 min.*

1⅓ cups balsamic vinegar
½ cup olive oil
½ cup sliced garlic chives
⅓ cup each *chopped shallots*
  and chopped fresh basil
1½ Tbsp. fresh thyme
1 Tbsp. chopped fresh oregano
1 tsp. chopped fresh rosemary
4 zucchini, sliced
6 large ears corn
4 each *unpeeled red onions*
  and large Asian eggplants,
  halved lengthwise
8 large fresh shiitake mushrooms
8 thin-skinned potatoes,
  boiled, halved
5 large red bell peppers
2¼ cups each *cooked wild rice*
  and brown rice
Salt and pepper
2 cups cherry tomatoes

In a nonreactive bowl, combine vinegar, oil, garlic chives, shallots, basil, thyme, oregano, and rosemary.

If desired, run thin wooden skewers through zucchini slices to hold flat. Place zucchini, corn, onions, eggplants, mushrooms, potatoes, and 4 peppers on a grill 4 to 6 inches above a solid bed of hot coals. Cook, turning until vegetables are browned and cooked through. Remove from grill; set aside.

Halve and seed grilled peppers. Cut kernels off 5 ears of corn; add to rice. Stem, seed, and dice remaining raw bell pepper and add to rice with 1½ cups herb dressing, and salt and pepper to taste; mix well.

Mound rice salad on a large platter. Surround with grilled vegetables and drizzle with any remaining dressing; garnish with remaining ear of corn and tomatoes.

Makes 8 servings

Index